Why is the sky blue?

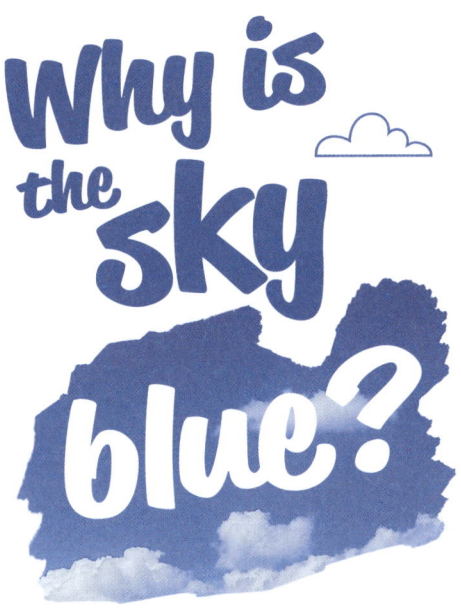

Why is the sky blue?

Hawys Morgan

Collins

Contents

Chapter 1 Why is the sea salty? 7

Bonus Earth myths. 20

Chapter 2 How do fish breathe? 23

Bonus The Ocean Cleanup 36

Chapter 3 Why is Earth round? 39

Bonus Our solar system 52

Chapter 4 Why do volcanoes erupt?. 55

Bonus Top volcanoes! 68

Chapter 5 Why is the sky blue?. 71

Bonus Glowing nature 86

Chapter 6 Why does the Moon change shape? . . 89

Glossary 104

About the author. 106

Book chat 108

Chapter 1
Why is the sea salty?

From the salty seas to the dusty desert, every living thing needs at least some water to survive.

If you go swimming in the sea, the water tastes salty. After your swim, you might even see traces of white salt on your skin and towel as they dry. This doesn't happen when you swim in a lake or a river. So why is the sea salty, but other water isn't?

Blue planet

An astronaut looking down at Earth from space would see a planet of swirling clouds, green and yellow land and *lots* of blue ocean! Water is one of the things that makes Earth a very special planet. Other planets in our **solar system** are made of rock or gases. Earth is the only planet which has large quantities of liquid water – that we know of, anyway! Maybe one day scientists will discover another watery planet like Earth.

Salty seas

Most of the water on Earth is salty, but where does that salt come from?

It mostly comes from rocks on land. Rocks naturally contain salt. Rain very slowly breaks down the rocks. The rainwater carries tiny amounts of salt from the rocks into streams and rivers. River water doesn't taste salty because the amounts are so small. This water flows downriver and ends up in the sea.

The sun heats up the surface of the sea. Some water **evaporates**, leaving any salt behind. In this way, salt gradually builds up in the sea. Scientists think about four billion tons of salt enters the sea every year – that's a lot of salt!

1. The sun heats the water.

4. Rain falls on rocks.

3. Clouds form.

2. Water evaporates, but salt stays in the sea.

5. Salt from rocks flows to the sea.

Another source of salt in seawater is from the seafloor. Salty pillars of rock in the sea that formed millions of years ago gradually dissolve into the water. Underwater volcanoes and **vents** also make the sea salty.

Heat from the volcanoes and vents causes chemical reactions that release salt from rocks underwater. Some underwater volcanoes will be erupting right now. In fact, about three-quarters of all volcanic activity on Earth happens deep underwater.

Let's find out more about salty water on our planet.

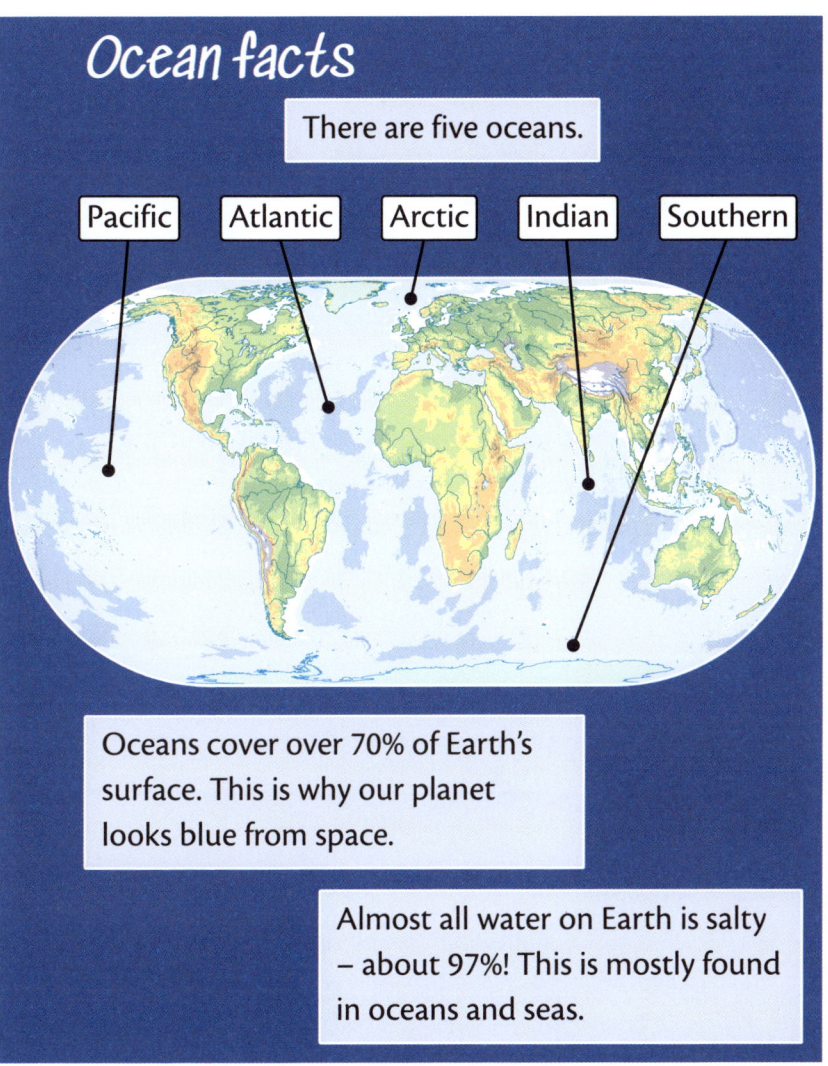

Ocean facts

There are five oceans.

Pacific Atlantic Arctic Indian Southern

Oceans cover over 70% of Earth's surface. This is why our planet looks blue from space.

Almost all water on Earth is salty – about 97%! This is mostly found in oceans and seas.

How did the Dead Sea get its name?

If you've ever been swimming in the sea, then you may have noticed that it's easier to float in than in a swimming pool filled with fresh water. This is because salt makes the water denser. That means it's more able to support the weight of people, animals and other items. As a result, things can float more easily in the sea than in **freshwater**.

The Dead Sea is a salt lake in a desert in the Middle East. Millions of years ago, it was part of the sea, but over time, changes to the landscape cut it off from the sea and it became a very salty lake.

The Dead Sea is exceptionally salty because of its location. It hardly ever rains in the desert, so the lake is mainly topped up by water from the River Jordan. This river water contains some salt from rocks too. Once this water enters the lake, there's nowhere else for it to go. The hot desert sun evaporates the water, leaving behind the salt that keeps building up in and around the lake. There is very little rain to **dilute** this saltwater which is why the Dead Sea is so salty.

Because the Dead Sea is extra salty, people float effortlessly on its surface. It's almost impossible to sink in the Dead Sea. It's about ten times saltier than most oceans.

On the downside, it's so salty, hardly anything can survive in the water. People do swim in it but they should wear long swimming costumes and goggles to protect their skin and eyes from the salt.

Less salty seas

Water in the sea is less salty at the North and South **poles**. This is because ice and icebergs are made of frozen freshwater, not saltwater. Freshwater from melting ice mixes with the seawater, diluting it, and so this makes the sea at the poles less salty.

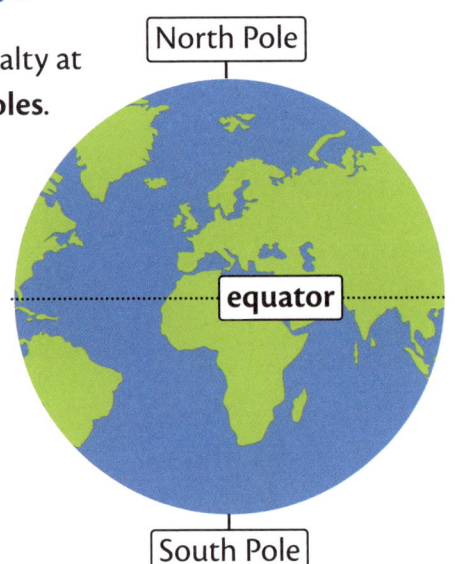

Seawater is also less salty at the equator. This is because it rains more at the equator and when this rain falls into the ocean it mixes with the seawater, making it less salty.

Water and our bodies

> Water, water everywhere but not a drop to drink!

This expression describes being at sea, surrounded by water, but as it is saltwater, there's nothing to drink. Humans can only drink freshwater.

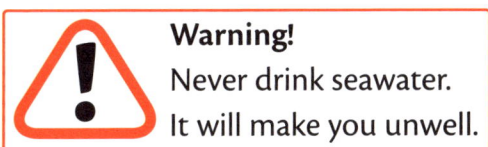

Warning!
Never drink seawater.
It will make you unwell.

Only 3% of water on Earth is freshwater. Some of Earth's freshwater is found in rivers, lakes and streams. Most freshwater is locked up in ice and **glaciers** or is hidden underground.

We lose water when we sweat, breathe and go to the toilet. It's important to drink plenty of water, especially when the weather is hot, or if you are doing lots of exercise.

Salty sweat

Have you ever noticed that sweat is a bit salty? Sweat is mostly water, but it also contains salt that is naturally in our bodies.

Sweating is one of the ways our bodies cool down when we are too hot. Sweat cools the skin as it evaporates.

Here are some other ways water helps your body to work properly:

- Water in your blood moves important things such as nutrients and a gas called **oxygen** around your body. About half your blood is made up of water. There is also salt in blood!

- Water in your urine (wee) helps to get rid of waste in your body.

- Water creates a cushion between your brain and your skull, protecting your brain from harm.

Humans are approximately 60% water. That's nearly two-thirds of your body. A baby is 78% water! Some foods, like cucumber and lettuce, are a whopping 95% water!

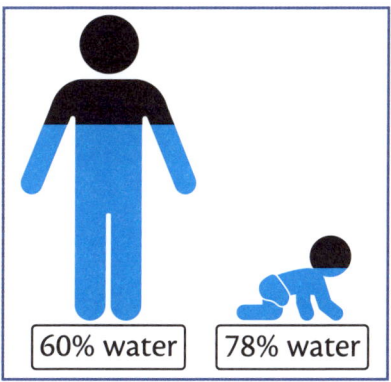

Like humans, many land animals can only drink freshwater. Other animals can *only* live in saltwater. Their bodies have developed ways to pump out the salt, so they don't get sick.

If plants don't get enough water, they begin to droop, and their leaves turn brown. Eventually, the plant will die. Most plants can't survive in saltwater. Some plants, like mangroves, can survive because they have special roots that filter salt out of seawater.

Water is precious. We must keep our lakes, rivers and seas clean, and we shouldn't waste water. It's up to us all to protect Earth's water – salty and fresh – so all living things on our blue planet have what they need to survive.

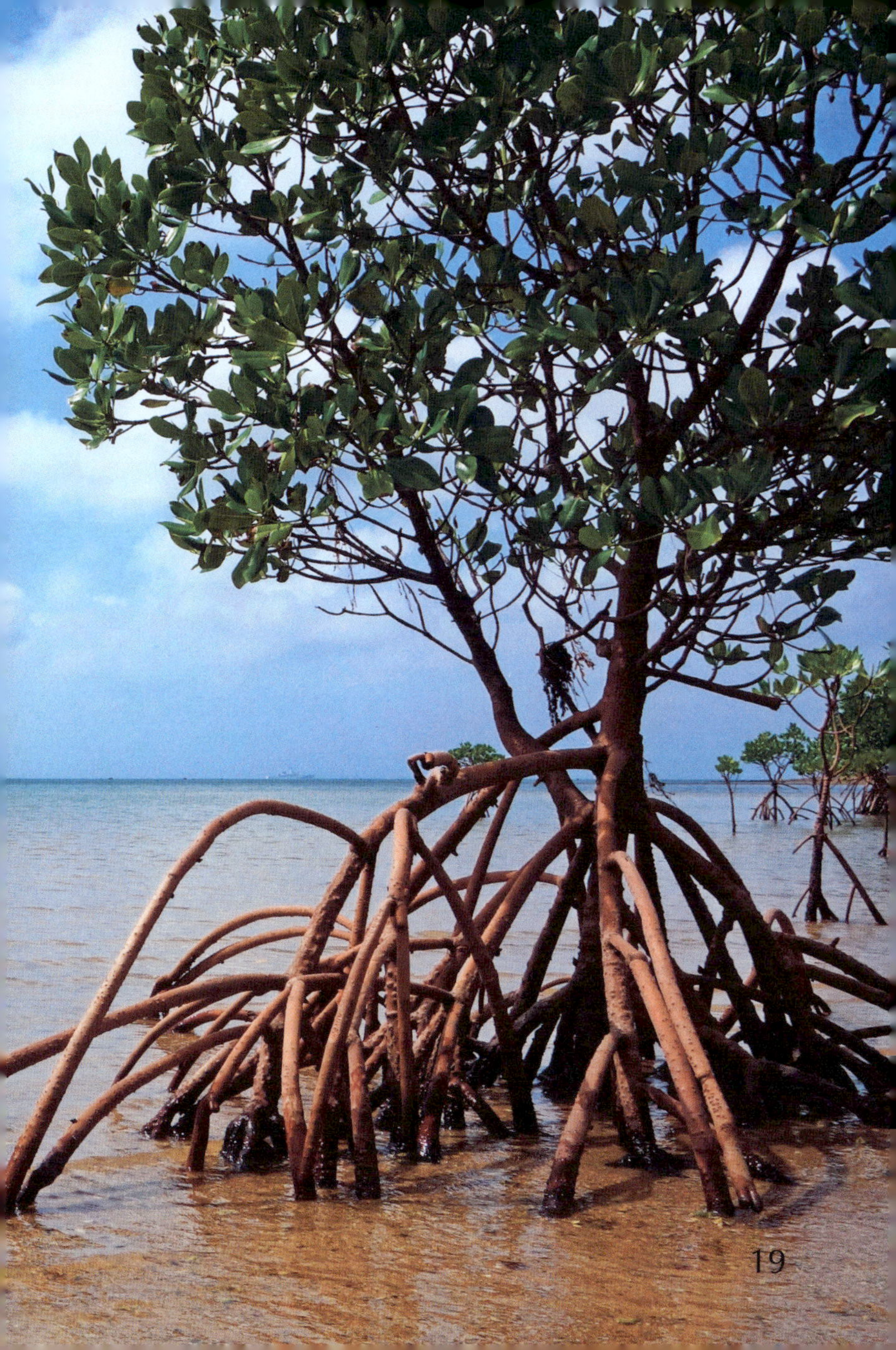

Bonus

Earth myths

1 All deserts are hot.

Wrong! Deserts can be scorching hot. However, deserts can also be freezing cold. A desert is simply a place where it doesn't rain much. Atacama and Antarctica are both deserts.

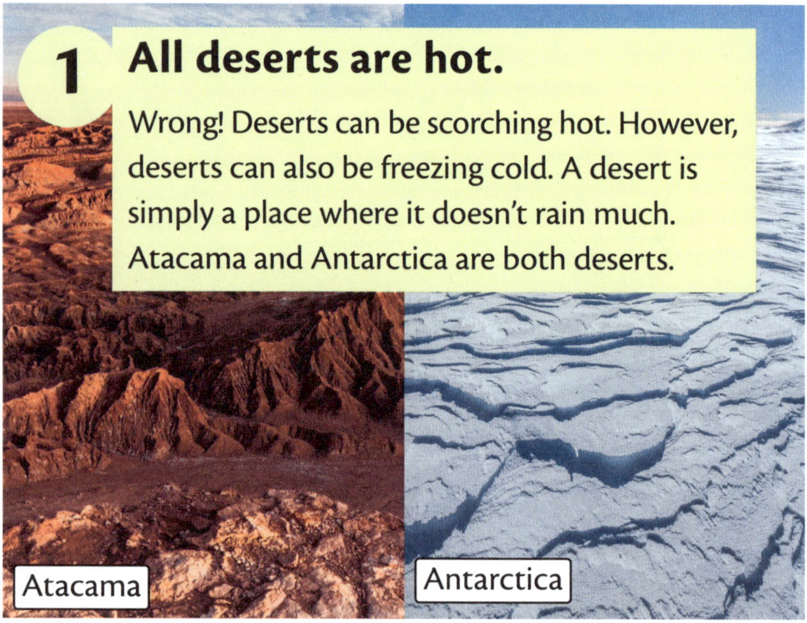
Atacama
Antarctica

2 Earth is solid.

Actually, Earth isn't completely solid – it's squishy inside! That's because of the high temperatures and strong pressure deep inside Earth.

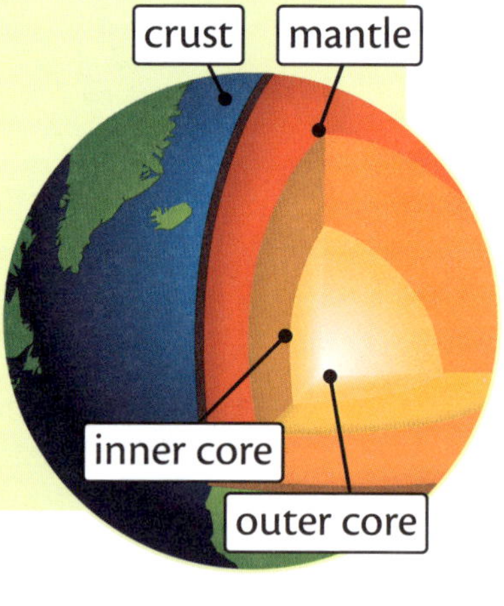
crust
mantle
inner core
outer core

3 Everest is the highest mountain on Earth.

Well … Everest is *one of* the highest mountains on Earth. However, Mauna Kea in Hawaii is technically taller by over a kilometre. It's over ten kilometres tall, but its base is hidden under the ocean so only four kilometres of the mountain is above sea level.

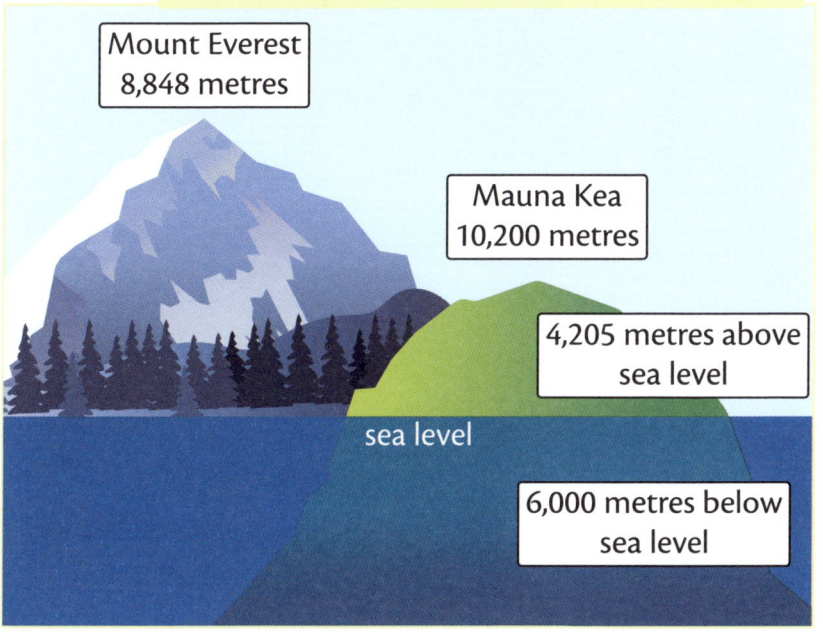

Chapter 2

How do fish breathe?

You're diving into a swimming pool. Splash! Once underwater, you have to hold your breath until you come back up to the surface. This is because humans can't breathe in water. Fish, on the other hand, have no trouble doing this. Why can fish breathe under water when humans can't?

Almost all animals need oxygen to survive. Many animals get oxygen by breathing air. Unlike humans, fish get their oxygen from water, not air. Fish don't use lungs to breathe; they use gills. These are the little openings on either side of a fish's head.

How humans breathe

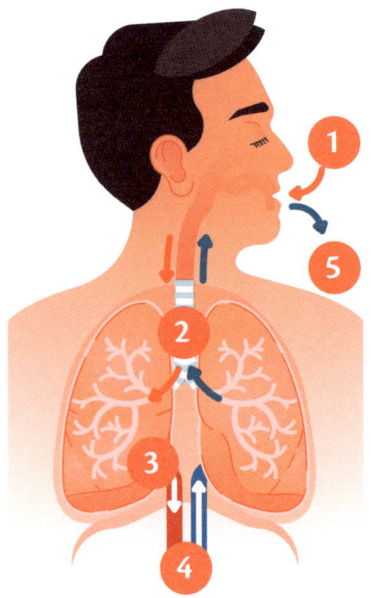

1. You take air into your body through your mouth and nose.
2. This air goes into your lungs.
3. Oxygen from the air passes through your lungs and into your blood.
4. Your blood carries oxygen around your body.
5. You breathe out air and waste **carbon dioxide**.

How fish breathe

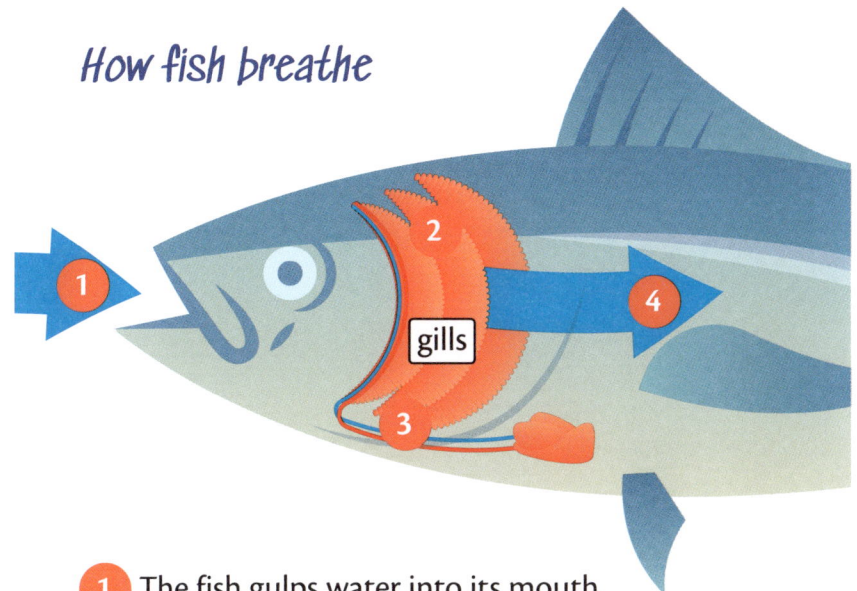

1. The fish gulps water into its mouth.
2. The water is pumped through the fish's gills.
3. Oxygen from the water passes through the gills into the fish's blood. That blood carries oxygen around the fish's body.
4. Water and waste carbon dioxide pass out of the fish through a bony flap near the gills.

Did you know?
Fish have lived on Earth for more than 450 million years!

Giant gills

Despite the name, whale sharks aren't whales at all. They're sharks, and all sharks are fish, unlike whales which are mammals. Whale sharks breathe through five pairs of huge gills.

These giant gills are part of the reason why whale sharks are the largest fish in the world. As well as being essential for breathing, these gills also help whale sharks to feed. Whale sharks gulp in water through their massive mouths. They filter food out of the seawater, a bit like a sieve. The water then escapes back through the gills.

This system means these sharks can eat a lot and breathe efficiently at the same time. As a result, they grow to large sizes.

On average, they are about 12 metres long – that's longer than a bus. The longest whale shark ever discovered was nearly 20 metres long. They are often called 'gentle giants' because, although they are big, they aren't dangerous. Divers and snorkellers can safely swim next to them.

Breaking the surface

Not all animals that live in water have gills. Animals like whales, dolphins and turtles breathe using lungs, just like humans.

Whales and dolphins breathe through a hole called a blowhole on top of their heads. A blowhole works in a similar way to our nostrils. When whales come up to the surface of the sea, they take a breath through their blowhole. After taking the breath, the blowhole seals itself tightly again so water can't get into the whales' lungs.

Dolphins break out of the water to breathe (sometimes jumping quite high). As they surface, they breathe out before they breathe in fresh air. As they breathe out, they spray water out of the top of their blowhole. Dolphins usually take a breath every four or five minutes.

Whales that dive deep in the sea can wait over an hour before they need to take a breath. So how can whales hold their breath for so long?

Whales don't only store oxygen in their lungs. They can store large quantities of oxygen in their blood and muscles too.

Whales also have some energy-saving tricks that help their stores of oxygen last. They can make their hearts beat slower. They can even stop blood from flowing to certain parts of the body. This reduces how much oxygen their bodies use.

Turtles

Turtles don't have blowholes *or* gills. So how do they breathe in the water? Mostly, they breathe in a similar way to humans – through their mouths and into their lungs. They have very large lungs that can store lots of oxygen, so sea turtles can spend several hours under water before needing to come to the surface.

Some freshwater turtles even hibernate underwater in winter. So, how do they get oxygen when they're sleeping for months at the bottom of a lake? They use a rather surprising part of their bodies … their bottoms! These turtles have a special hole near their tails which can take oxygen directly from the water. They don't need to use their lungs for this. They can't take in much oxygen this way, but it's enough to see them through the slow, sleepy winter months.

The best of both worlds

Some animals, such as frogs, can live both on land and in water. We call this kind of animal an amphibian.

When frog eggs hatch, they turn into tadpoles. Tadpoles have gills like a fish. When they grow into froglets, they lose their gills and develop lungs. Adult frogs also have skin that is so thin, it can absorb oxygen from water. So, frogs can breathe through their skin underwater, and out of water they can use both their skin and their lungs. They don't need gills.

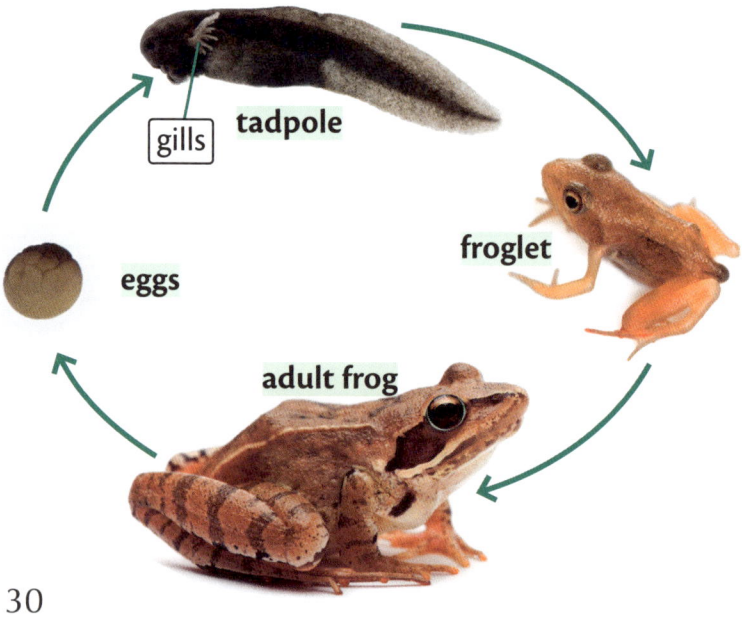

Did you know?

Axolotls (say *ax/o/lot/l*) are amphibians too. Axolotls are special because they have gills, lungs *and* they can breathe through their skin. They also have an unusual superpower – they can regrow body parts! If axolotls lose a leg, or even suffer damage to their heart or brain, they can regrow it. Amazing!

Extreme explorers

Despite not being able to breathe underwater, humans can explore the sea with the help of technology. In fairly shallow water, scuba divers can carry tanks of air that they breathe using a special mask. This enables them to stay underwater for longer periods, observing the world around them.

However, the deep sea is a much trickier place to explore. It isn't safe for humans to dive in deep water. This is because the deeper you go, the more pressure there is.

One of the deepest parts of the ocean is the Mariana Trench, in the Pacific Ocean, south of Japan. At the bottom of it, the pressure is the equivalent of 100 elephants standing on your head!

Pressure

Air pressure is the weight of air pressing on us. We don't notice it because we are used to it. There is water pressure too. This is the weight of water pressing on us. Water pressure is stronger than air pressure, and it gets stronger and stronger the deeper underwater we go.

Mariana Trench depth of 11 kilometres →

For a long time, scientists thought nothing could live in the Mariana Trench because of the dark, the cold and the pressure. Thanks to deep-sea cameras and driverless submarines, we now know that there is plenty of life in there. There are footballfish, vampire squid, dumbo octopuses and goblin sharks. These animals have adapted to live with the massive pressure, cold and darkness.

Scientists have found more than just unusual animals at the bottom of the Mariana Trench. They have also found plastic. Sadly, even this remote place isn't safe from rubbish.

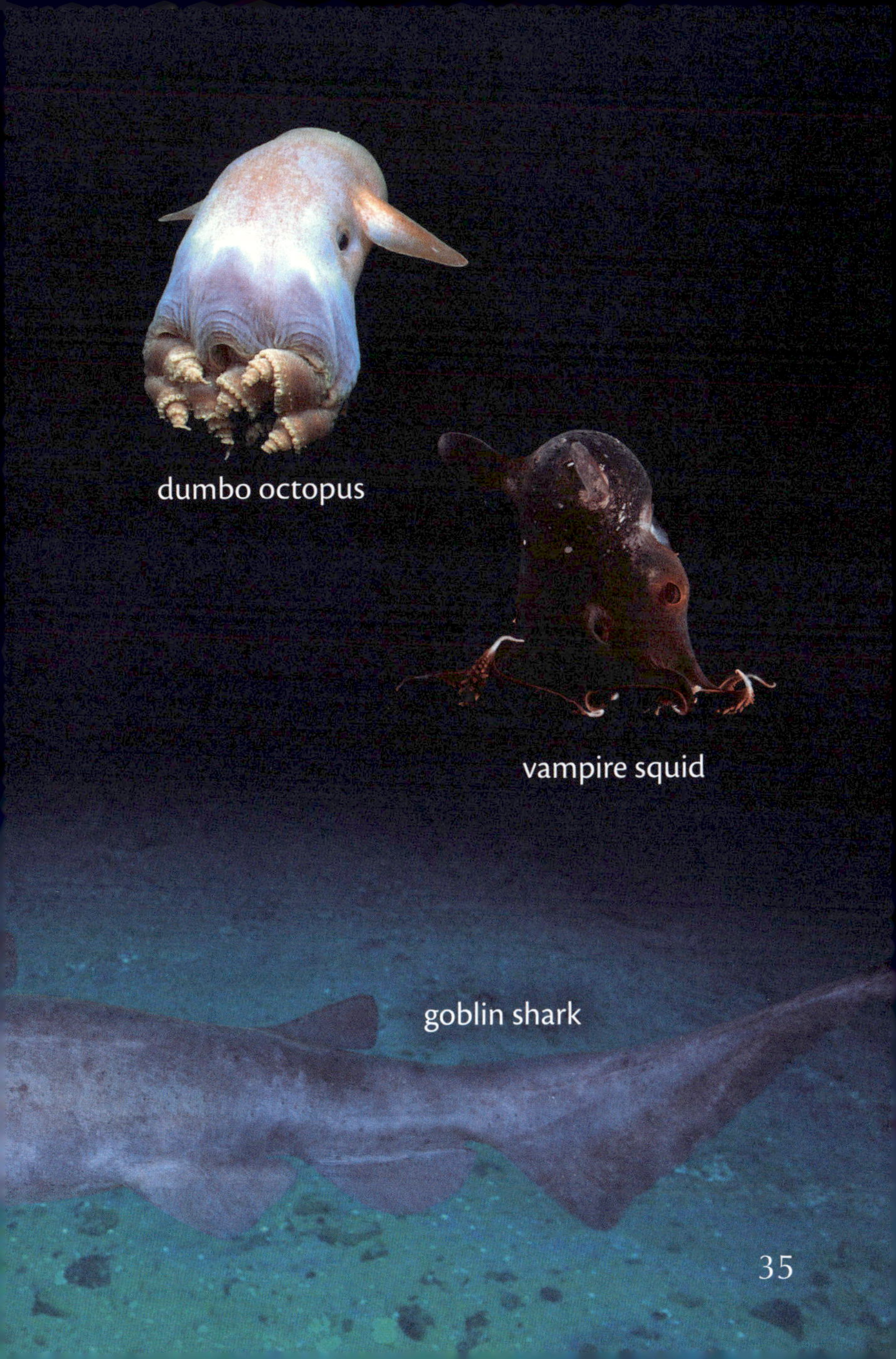
dumbo octopus
vampire squid
goblin shark

Bonus

The Ocean Cleanup

When Boyan Slat was 16, he went scuba diving. Sadly, he saw more plastic bags than fish. Two years later, in 2013, he set up an organisation called The Ocean Cleanup.

Trillions of pieces of plastic pollute Earth's oceans harming plants, animals and people. The Ocean Cleanup develops technology that can remove plastic from our rivers and oceans.

The Ocean Cleanup aims to remove 90% of floating plastic pollution by 2040.

The amount of rubbish removed by The Ocean Cleanup in just one year:

11 million kilos

How can you help?

- Take part in a litter pick.
- Put your rubbish in the bin.
- Use reusable shopping bags and water bottles.
- Try to reduce single-use plastic where you can.

Chapter 3
Why is Earth round?

When you're doing an everyday activity like playing in the playground or eating a snack, it's easy to forget that we live on a planet circling around a huge star in a solar system.

Flat Earth

Hundreds of years ago, people didn't know that Earth was round. Many people assumed it was flat. The ancient Egyptians thought Earth was a disc in an ocean. The Vikings had a similar idea, but they believed there was a giant tree in the middle of the disc. In ancient China, people thought Earth was flat and square.

At first, the ancient Greeks thought the world was a flat disc on top of a cylinder. Then around 500 BCE, an ancient Greek called Pythagoras worked out that the moon was a **sphere**. He had the idea that if the moon was spherical, then Earth was probably a similar shape too. By observing the movement of planets and stars in the sky, other ancient Greek thinkers were able to prove that Earth was a sphere.

a statue of Pythagoras

Nowadays, we don't even need to do any complicated science experiments to prove that Earth is a sphere. Photos taken by astronauts at the International Space Station show that it is sphere-shaped. In fact, all planets are 'near-spheres', whether they are made of rock or gas. They are called near-spheres because they're not all perfectly round. But why is that? Why isn't Earth shaped like a cube? Why isn't Mars pyramid-shaped?

Gravity glue

Planets are spheres because of an invisible force called **gravity**. This force holds things together in space, including planets. Gravity pulls smaller objects towards larger objects.

A planet's gravity pulls objects towards its centre – this kind of gravity is called self-gravity. If an object in space is large enough, this self-gravity pulls equally from all sides. This is what creates the sphere shape. For example, a planet like Mars is made of bits of rock and dust. Gravity pulls all those bits of rock and dust, and everything else that the planet is made of, towards the centre of the planet. Gravity holds all that rock and dust together, a bit like glue.

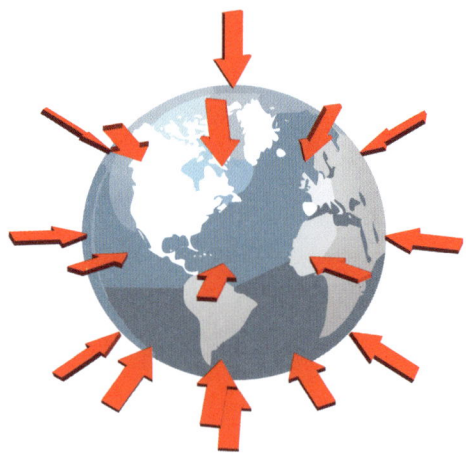

We can thank gravity for making our planet spherical. But did you know that without gravity, Earth wouldn't exist at all? When our sun first formed, clouds of gas and dust swirled around it. This gas and dust collided and grouped together, eventually forming planets, including our planet. Gravity held that gas and dust together.

Did you know?

Earth first formed 4.6 billion years ago. It took a little while longer for life to exist on Earth. Scientists think life on Earth began about 3.8 billion years ago.

Some planets are more sphere-like than others. Mercury and Venus are almost perfect spheres. Saturn and Jupiter bulge around the middle. But how round is Earth? The answer involves rotation!

All planets spin around and around, a bit like when someone spins a basketball on one finger. This is called rotation.

You may have experienced rotation at the playground or funfair. On some big fairground rides, when you spin around very fast, the rotation flings you outwards.

Although gravity holds Earth together, rotation causes some of the material the planet is made of to bulge out. It makes a slight bulge around the middle of the planet.

So, now we know that Earth is round because of gravity. Gravity has another important function in our solar system. Thanks to Earth's gravity, we don't float away into space. Gravity holds our planet together by pulling everything towards the centre, and it's that same force that pulls us towards the ground and stops us floating away. It's the reason why any dropped item naturally falls towards the ground.

Gravity is also one of the reasons why planets move around the Sun in a big oval-shaped path called an **orbit**.

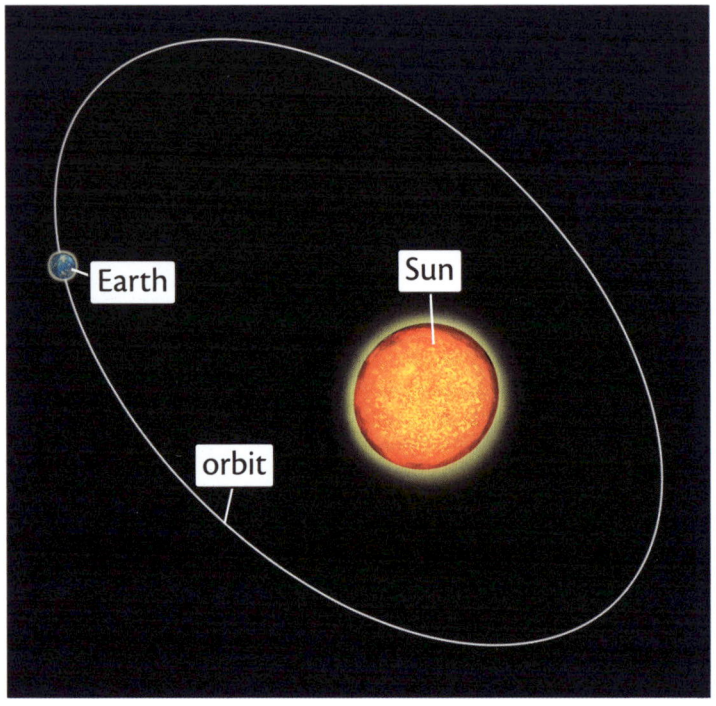

The Sun's gravity pulls all the planets in our solar system towards its centre. So, why don't all the planets just crash into the Sun?

It's all about movement

The planets don't crash into the Sun because they're moving so quickly. Without the Sun's gravity, in theory, planets would move through space in a straight line forever. However, the Sun's gravity is always pulling the planets back towards it. There is a constant push and pull between a planet wanting to travel in a straight line and the Sun's gravity pulling the planet towards the centre of the Sun. Because this push and pull is balanced, planets travel in an orbit around the Sun.

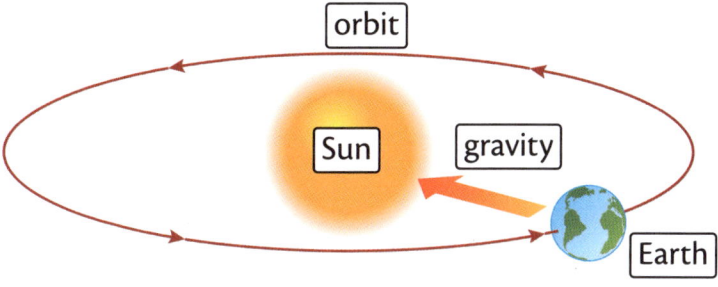

We now know a little about how Earth was formed and why it is round. We know that Earth is our planet, but have you ever wondered what a planet actually is?

There are three key things that make a planet a planet.

1. A planet must orbit around a star. In our solar system, this star is the Sun.
2. It must be big enough for gravity to have squeezed it into a sphere-shape.
3. It must be the biggest object in its orbit around the sun – this means it has either swept away other objects, such as rock or ice, or absorbed them. Pluto isn't a planet because it is smaller than other objects in its orbit.

Earth is the third planet from the Sun. There are eight planets in our solar system. The four planets closest to the Sun (Mercury, Venus, Earth and Mars) are made from rock and metal. The four planets furthest from the Sun are Jupiter, Saturn, Uranus and Neptune. They are mostly made of gases.

A perfect planet

Earth has some things in common with the other planets in our solar system, such as its shape and its orbit around the Sun. However, in other ways it is very different. One thing that makes Earth special is that it is the only planet in our solar system with liquid water on the surface. Other planets have ice and water vapour, but not liquid water. Without this water, life on Earth would not be possible.

Another thing that makes life on Earth possible is Earth's **atmosphere**.

Here are some of the reasons that atmosphere is important:

- It contains the air that we need to breathe. It's a special mix of gases that all living things need to survive.
- Changes in the atmosphere cause weather, such as rain, snow, wind and storms.
- The atmosphere helps to keep the planet at the right temperature for life to exist.
- Earth's atmosphere acts like a shield, protecting Earth from being hit by bits of rock travelling through space.

What stops Earth's atmosphere from floating off? You guessed it – gravity! Earth's gravity keeps the atmosphere in place.

Thanks to gravity, this spinning sphere that we live on is a pretty perfect planet!

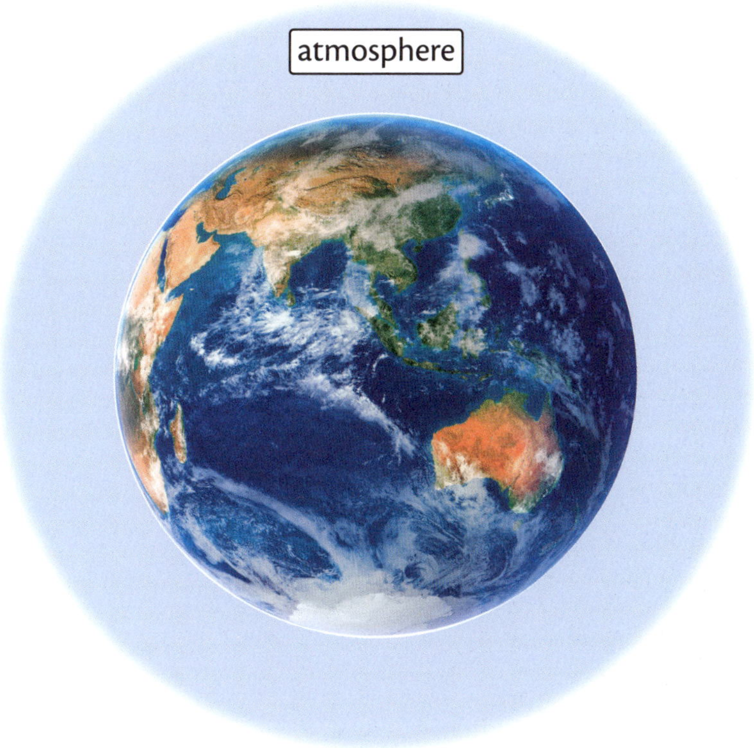
atmosphere

Our solar system

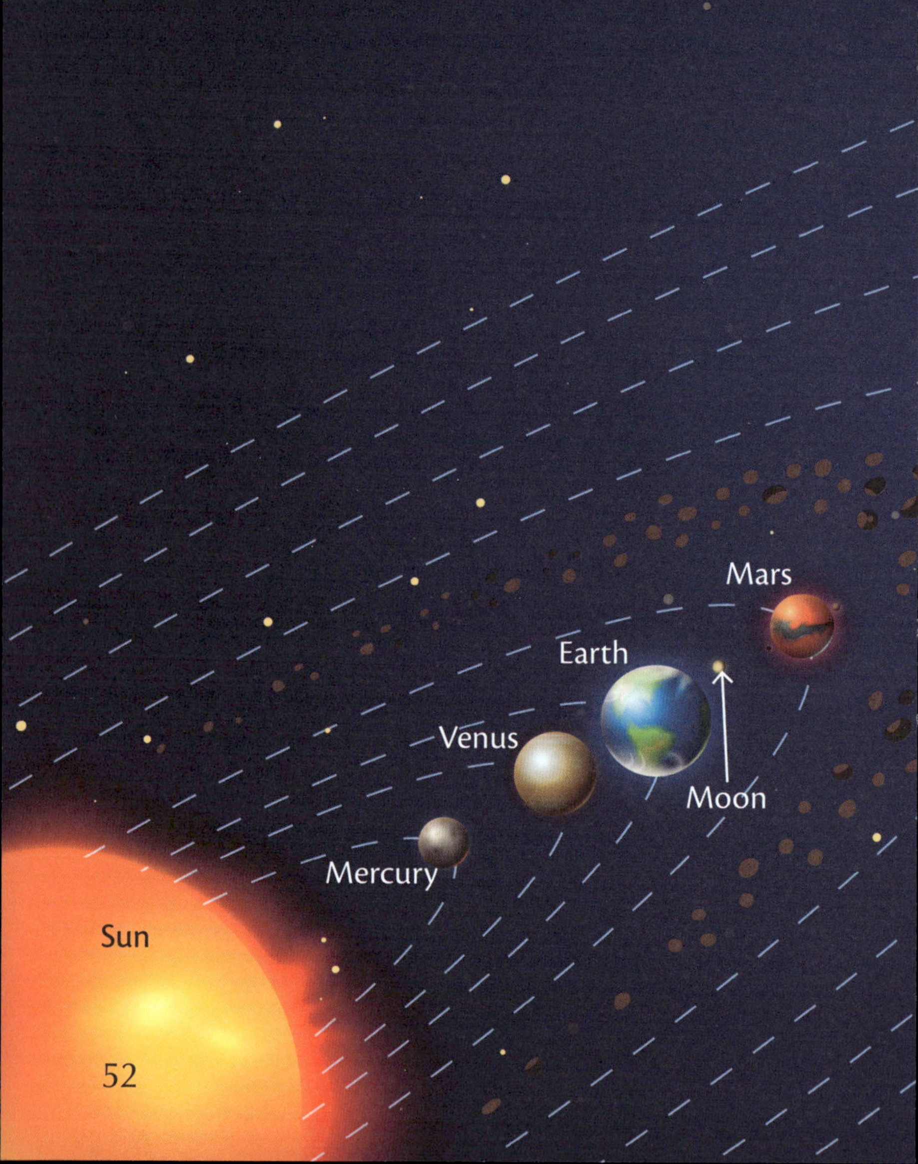
Mars
Earth
Moon
Venus
Mercury
Sun

Neptune

Uranus

Saturn

Jupiter

Chapter 4

Why do volcanoes erupt?

The ground underneath us may look solid and peaceful, but beneath Earth's surface, things are pretty lively.

A journey to the centre of Earth

Earth is made up of layers. We live on Earth's surface. This top layer of Earth is called the crust – like the crunchy outside of a loaf of bread. It's the thinnest layer.

The next layer is called the mantle. This is a mix of solid and melted rock.

At the very centre of Earth is the inner core. This is a huge, scorching-hot metal sphere – the temperature is around 5,000–6,000 degrees Celsius. That's about the same temperature as the surface of the Sun!

Structure of Earth

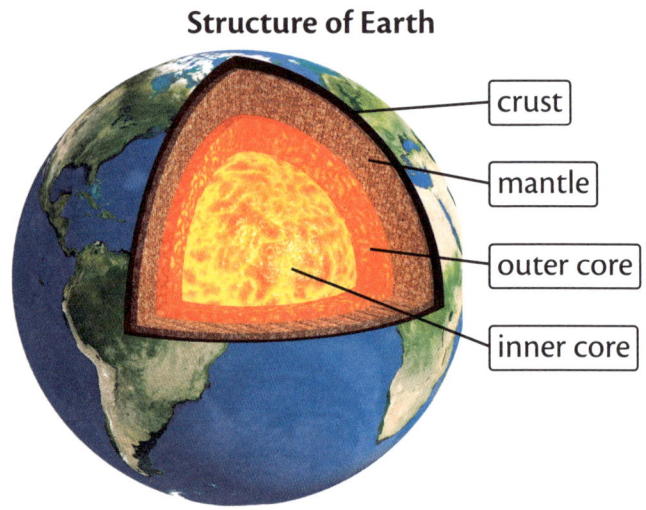

A volcano gives us a window into the planet beneath our feet. When a volcano erupts, hot ash, gases and molten rock called **magma** escape from the mantle through cracks in Earth's crust. Volcanoes are a dramatic reminder of the red-hot heart of our planet.

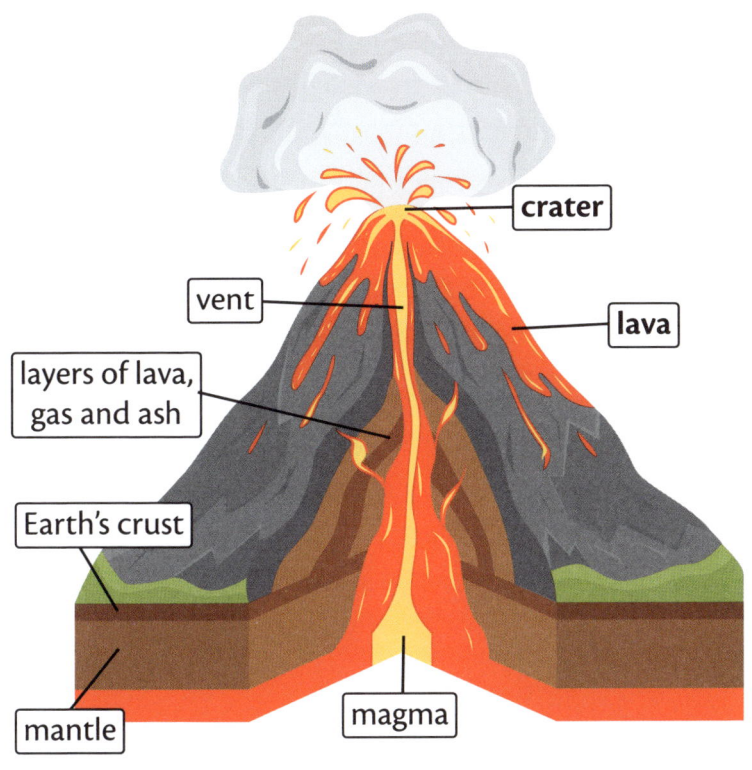

When a volcano erupts, ash and poisonous gases are spewed into the air. Magma squeezes up through Earth's crust. Once magma emerges onto Earth's surface, we call it lava, not magma. Lava can flow from a volcano in fiery slow rivers, or can catapult from it in big burning lumps called lava bombs.

There are three main categories of volcanoes that you might see on Earth:

1. Active volcanoes that may erupt at any time.
2. Dormant volcanoes that aren't active now, but could become active at some point.
3. Extinct volcanoes that were active in the past but won't erupt again.

How many active volcanoes do you think there are on Earth? Maybe 15? Or 150? In fact, scientists think there are around 1,500 active volcanoes on Earth.

A jigsaw puzzle

Volcanic eruptions usually happen along the edges of Earth's tectonic plates. These are big slabs of Earth's crust and mantle that fit together like a huge jigsaw. There are seven massive tectonic plates, ten large plates and many smaller ones.

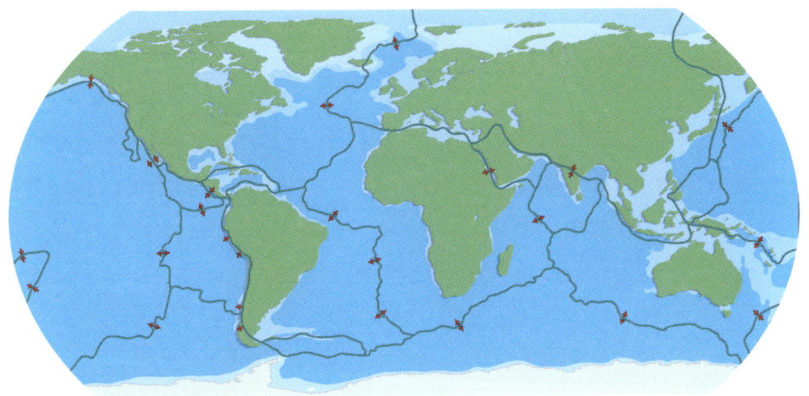

Underneath the tectonic plates, there is a layer of magma. The tectonic plates sit on top of this and are always moving. They move so slowly that we can't feel the movement. Sometimes they move apart, sometimes they bump into each other and sometimes they slide past each other.

Volcanoes don't form when tectonic plates slide past each other, but they do form when tectonic plates move towards or away from each other.

Did you know?
Most earthquakes also occur where tectonic plates meet.

How volcanoes form

Magma is most likely to find its way to the surface when the tectonic plates are moving away from each other. When Earth's crust moves apart, a new gap for rising magma to come to the surface is created.

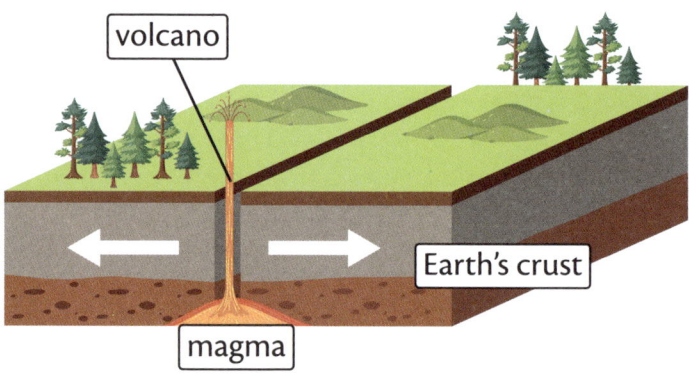

When tectonic plates move towards each other, they collide, and one plate is forced under the other. The plate that's pushed under sinks into Earth's mantle, and then the rock of that plate melts and forms magma. The pressure of this magma builds and builds under Earth's surface until it suddenly erupts. These volcanic eruptions can be very dramatic.

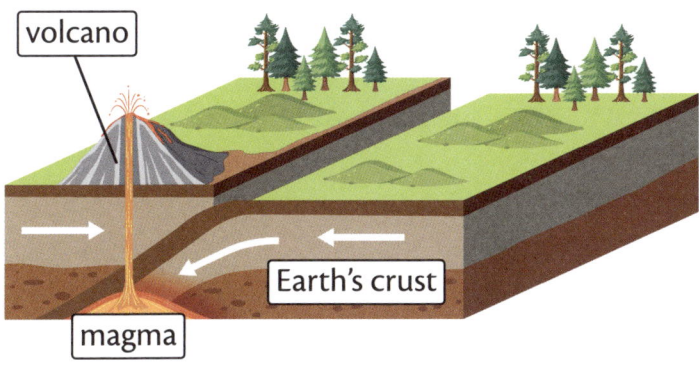

Volcanic eruptions can destroy towns, kill animals and plants, and even change the climate.

In 1815, a volcano called Mount Tambora in Indonesia erupted. It was one of the most powerful eruptions of the last 10,000 years!

It threw up a massive cloud of ash into the air, so huge that it blocked sunlight. For months, temperatures around the world were lower than normal because of this. It affected people as far away as Europe and North America. It even snowed in mid-summer!

More than three-quarters of Earth's volcanoes are dotted around the edges of the Pacific tectonic plate. This huge circle of about 452 volcanoes is called the Ring of Fire! Mount Tambora is one of these volcanoes.

The Ring of Fire

Pacific Ocean

Hotspots

Most volcanoes form around tectonic plates, but not all do. The Hawaiian Islands formed in the middle of the Pacific Ocean thanks to volcanic eruptions, but they are thousands of kilometres away from the nearest tectonic plate boundary.

Scientists think this chain of volcanoes was created in a 'hotspot'.

We don't know why these hotspots exist, yet. But we do know that they are fixed sections in the Earth's mantle where magma rises. And these hotspots can create a chain of volcanoes. Extremely hot magma from the hotspot melts Earth's crust and flows up to the surface, forming a volcano. Over time, the tectonic plate moves, taking the volcano away from the hotspot. Eventually, that volcano becomes extinct and new volcanoes form over the hotspot. This happens again and again, ending up with a chain of volcanoes.

Growing volcanoes

Some active volcanoes, like those in Hawaii, are always erupting. Lava flows from them gently and constantly. Runny lava and gases slowly ooze from these volcanoes over a large area, gradually forming a dome shape. Sometimes the lava dribbles into the sea where it quickly cools and hardens.

Arriving with a bang

Imagine a world without volcanoes – well, it would be very different! Around 2.2 billion years ago, Earth was mostly covered in water. Then … BOOM! Scientists believe there was a massive volcanic eruption of magma from under the surface of Earth. The lava cooled and hardened into land.

This formed a huge continuous area of land called a supercontinent. If it wasn't for that first volcanic eruption, there might not be land for us to live on.

Since then, land on Earth has broken up and then joined together again several times. Today, we don't have a supercontinent. Instead, we have seven **continents**: Europe, Africa, Asia, Australia, North America, South America and Antarctica.

Volcanoes still change our landscape. Layers of lava and ash cool and harden on top of each other. Over many years, these layers gradually increase the size of a volcano. Eruptions from underwater volcanoes can create new islands.

A natural water heater

Volcanoes aren't the only thing created by the heat and magma under Earth's crust. Much of the freshwater on Earth is underground. In some places, magma heats this underground water. A hot spring is a place where this warm water finds its way to the surface. Many of these steamy pools of water are in North America, Iceland and Japan.

Volcanic eruptions can be very dangerous, but they're not all bad. Over time, ash makes the soil around volcanoes excellent for growing food. We can also make clean energy from the heat produced by volcanic activity. It's called geothermal energy.

Although volcanoes can bring destruction, Earth, as we know it, wouldn't be the same without them!

> **Did you know?**
>
> Japanese snow monkeys have a clever way to survive the freezing cold winters of northern Japan. They hang out with each other in volcanic hot springs!

Bonus

Top volcanoes!

Krakatau
Indonesia

Height 285 metres
Eruption level 6
Fact: When Krakatau erupted in 1883, ash in the air blocked out sunlight. The whole region was plunged into darkness for two and a half days.

Mount Fuji
Japan

Height 3,776 metres
Eruption level 5
Fact: Mount Fuji has become one of the most famous volcanoes in the world because it features in many well-known pictures like *The Great Wave off Kanagawa*.

The Great Wave off Kanagawa,
by Katsushika Hokusai (around 1830–1832)

Tambora
Indonesia

Height 2,850 metres
Eruption level 8
Fact: Tambora erupted in 1815. It was the largest volcanic eruption ever recorded. The eruption was so big, it blew the volcano apart!

Mount Erebus
Antarctica

Height 3,794 metres
Eruption level 2
Fact: Mount Erebus is famous for its ice towers and ice caves made by hot gases that escape from the volcano, then suddenly cool.

Kilauea
Hawaii, USA

Height 1,222 metres
Eruption level 3
Fact: Hawaiian stories say that one of its craters is the home of Pele, the Hawaiian fire goddess. The name Kilauea means 'much spreading' in Hawaiian.

Vesuvius
Italy

Height 1,281 metres
Eruption level 5
Fact: When Mount Vesuvius erupted in 79 CE, the ancient Roman cities of Pompeii and Herculaneum were destroyed after they were buried in lava, ash and mud. These forgotten cities were discovered in the 1700s.

Chapter 5
Why is the sky blue?

The sun is shining. There isn't a cloud in the bright, blue sky. But why *is* the sky blue?

Why isn't it green? Or brown? Why does it have a colour at all?

To understand why the sky is blue during the day, we need to learn a bit more about what light is and how it moves.

What is light?

We need light to see the world around us. Light is a form of energy and it's the fastest thing in the **universe**. Light can travel around Earth 7.5 times in a single second! That's super-fast!

Daylight travels from the Sun, through space to our planet – Earth.

8 minutes
The time it takes for sunlight to travel from the Sun to us here on Earth.

All the colours of the rainbow

At night, the sky is black. It's only blue during daytime. During the day, most of our light comes from the Sun.

Sunlight looks white, but it actually contains all of the colours of the rainbow:

red, **orange**, **yellow**, **green**, **blue**, **indigo** and **violet**.

These seven colours make up the colour spectrum.

Bouncy light

So now we know that light travels quickly *and* is made up of different colours, but that still doesn't explain why the sky is blue rather than yellow or violet. Understanding how our eyes see colour can help us answer this big question.

Objects appear coloured because of the way light bounces off them.

Look at this red dot.

It absorbs every colour in the colour spectrum *except* red. It looks red because red light bounces off the dot and into your eyes.

Your eyes tell your brain that you can see a dot shape and that it is red.

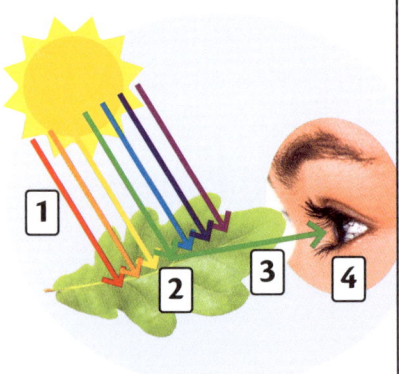

1. White light from the Sun shines on the leaf.

2. The leaf absorbs all the colours except green.

3. Green light bounces into your eyes.

4. Your eyes send a message to your brain that the leaf is green.

Wavy Light

Now we know why our eyes see certain colours when we look at the world around us. To understand why the sky looks blue and not another colour, we need to find out a bit about how the different colours of light travel from the Sun to Earth. Light travels in waves, a bit like waves in the sea.

Imagine a tropical beach with waves lapping gently at the shore. These are long, lazy waves. Then imagine the same beach after a jet ski has whizzed past. The waves aren't long and lazy anymore; they are short and choppy. **Light waves** are a bit like this.

Some light travels in long waves; other light travels in short waves. Red light has the longest waves. Violet light has the shortest waves. When light waves of all the colours travel together, the light looks white.

colour spectrum

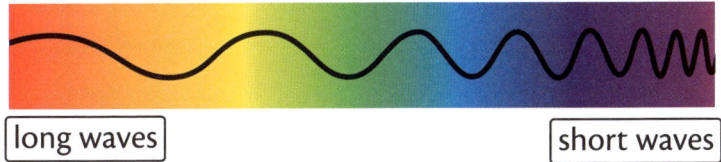

long waves   short waves

Sunlight travels from the Sun, through space, until it reaches Earth's atmosphere. The atmosphere sits like a big blanket of gases around the planet.

Most of the red, orange, yellow and green colours in light travel in long, lazy waves straight through Earth's atmosphere to our eyes. These waves travel together as a group and so the light looks more or less white to us.

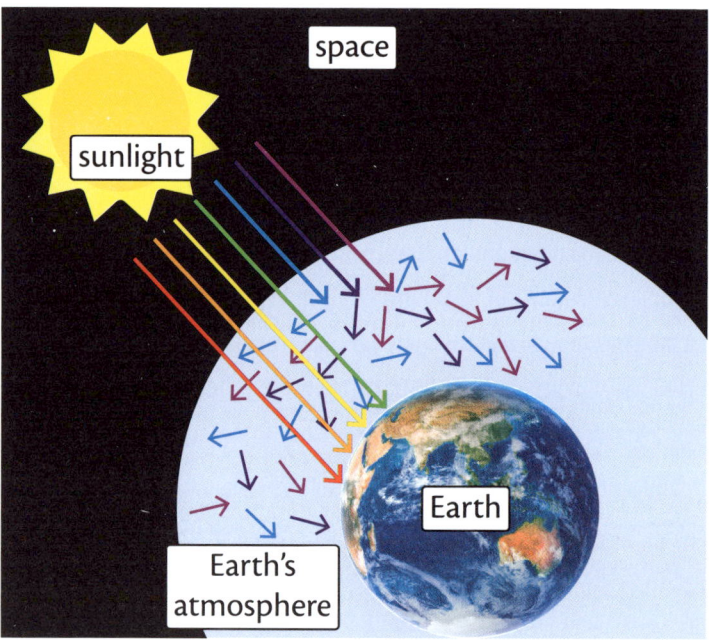

However, the blue, indigo and violet colours in light travel in short, choppy waves. These bounce off the different gases in Earth's atmosphere. So the blue, indigo and violet colours are separated from the rest of the light in the colour spectrum and get scattered in all directions.

The blue, indigo and violet light takes over the sky, making it look blue to our eyes. This is why the sky is blue during the day! Isn't it amazing to think of light moving in this way around us all of the time?

Did you know?

On Mars, the sky usually looks orange. This is because the atmosphere on Mars is different to Earth's atmosphere and light is scattered in a different way. Which sky do you prefer? Earth's blue sky or Mars' orange sky?

Now we understand why the sky usually looks blue, we can explore some of the other ways we see light on Earth.

Rainbows

A rainbow is a beautiful multicoloured arch in the sky. They are a common sight, but for thousands of years, people wondered what rainbows were and how they were formed. Some myths suggested rainbows were bridges between this world and other places. Thanks to the science of light, we now know the answer!

We mostly see rainbows when there's a mix of sun and rain showers. This is because most rainbows form when white light from the Sun strikes raindrops falling from clouds. The white light splits into all the colours of the colour spectrum.

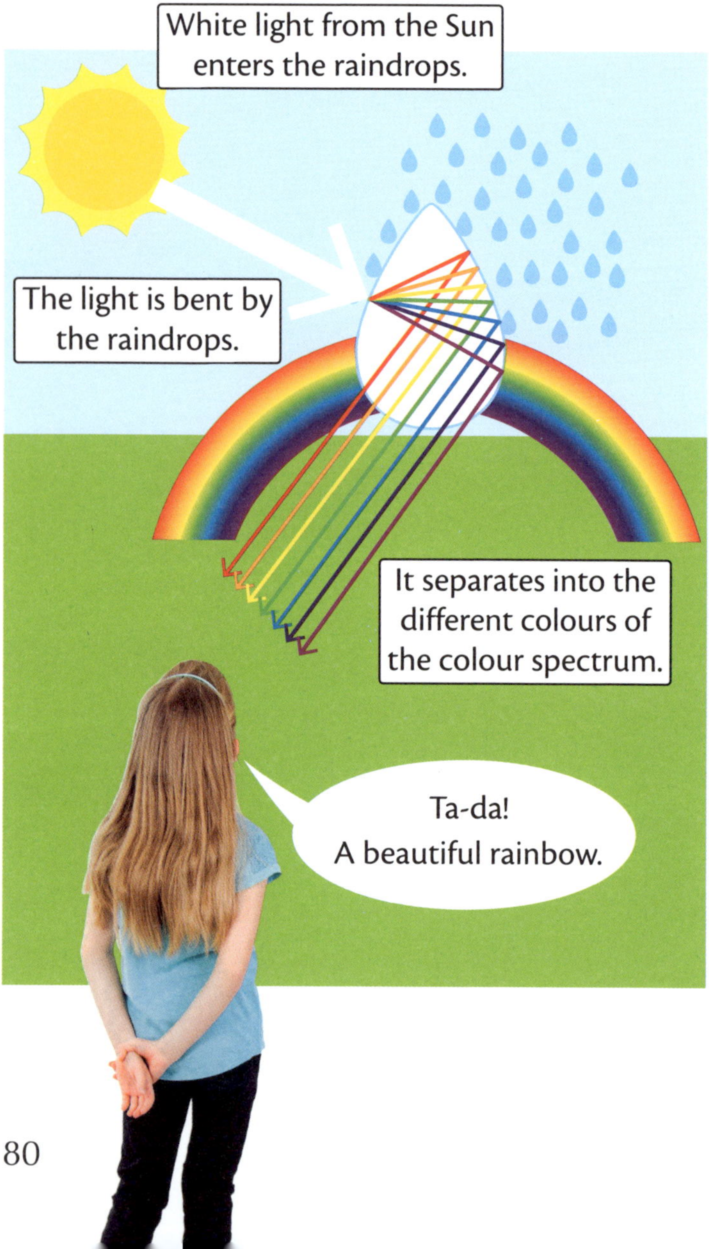
White light from the Sun enters the raindrops.
The light is bent by the raindrops.
It separates into the different colours of the colour spectrum.
Ta-da!
A beautiful rainbow.

It is possible to make your own rainbow. On a sunny day, stand outside with the sun behind you. Turn on a hose. Move the spray around in front of you until you see a rainbow form.

Did you know?

Rainbows aren't always arch-shaped. If you are high above land, for example, on a mountain top or in an aeroplane, you might see a rainbow that looks like a complete circle!

Black and white

At night, the sky no longer looks blue to us. Without light from the Sun, the sky looks black. This raises another interesting question: are black and white colours?

In one sense, they are colours. For example, you may find black and white in a box of colouring pencils.

However, scientifically, black and white aren't really colours.

We see white when an object reflects *all* the colours of the colour spectrum. Look at the white bits of this page. All the colours of the colour spectrum are bouncing back off the paper into your eyes, and your eyes tell your brain that the paper is white.

The opposite happens when we look at something black, like the words on this page. We see black when something absorbs all the colours of the colour spectrum. No colour is bounced into our eyes.

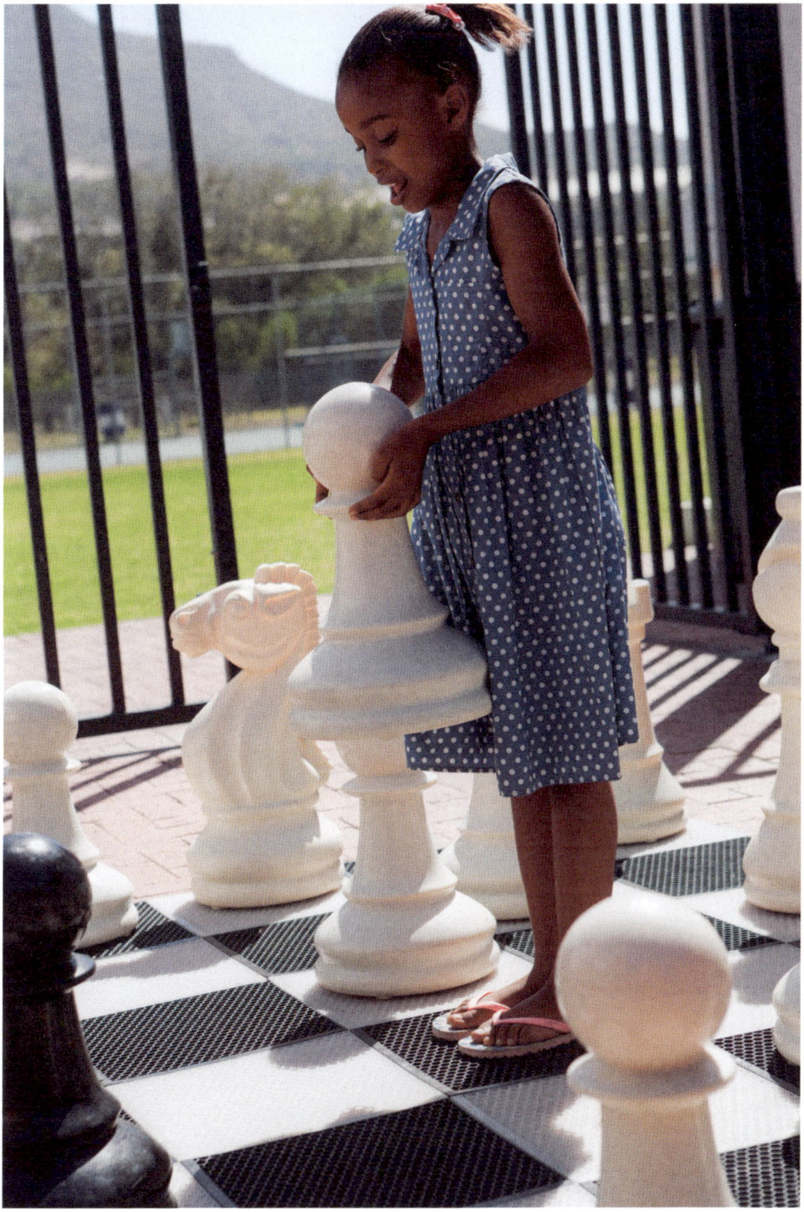

We don't all see the same thing

Some people find it difficult to tell the difference between colours because they can't see all the colours in the spectrum. This is called colour blindness or colour vision deficiency. If you are colour blind, it doesn't mean you can't see any colours. However, you may find it difficult to tell the difference between colours like oranges and yellows, and blues and purples. Colour blindness is quite common. There are probably several children with colour blindness in your school.

Whether or not you're colour blind, every time you look at the world around you, your eyes are sending millions of colour messages to your brain. Our bodies are amazing!

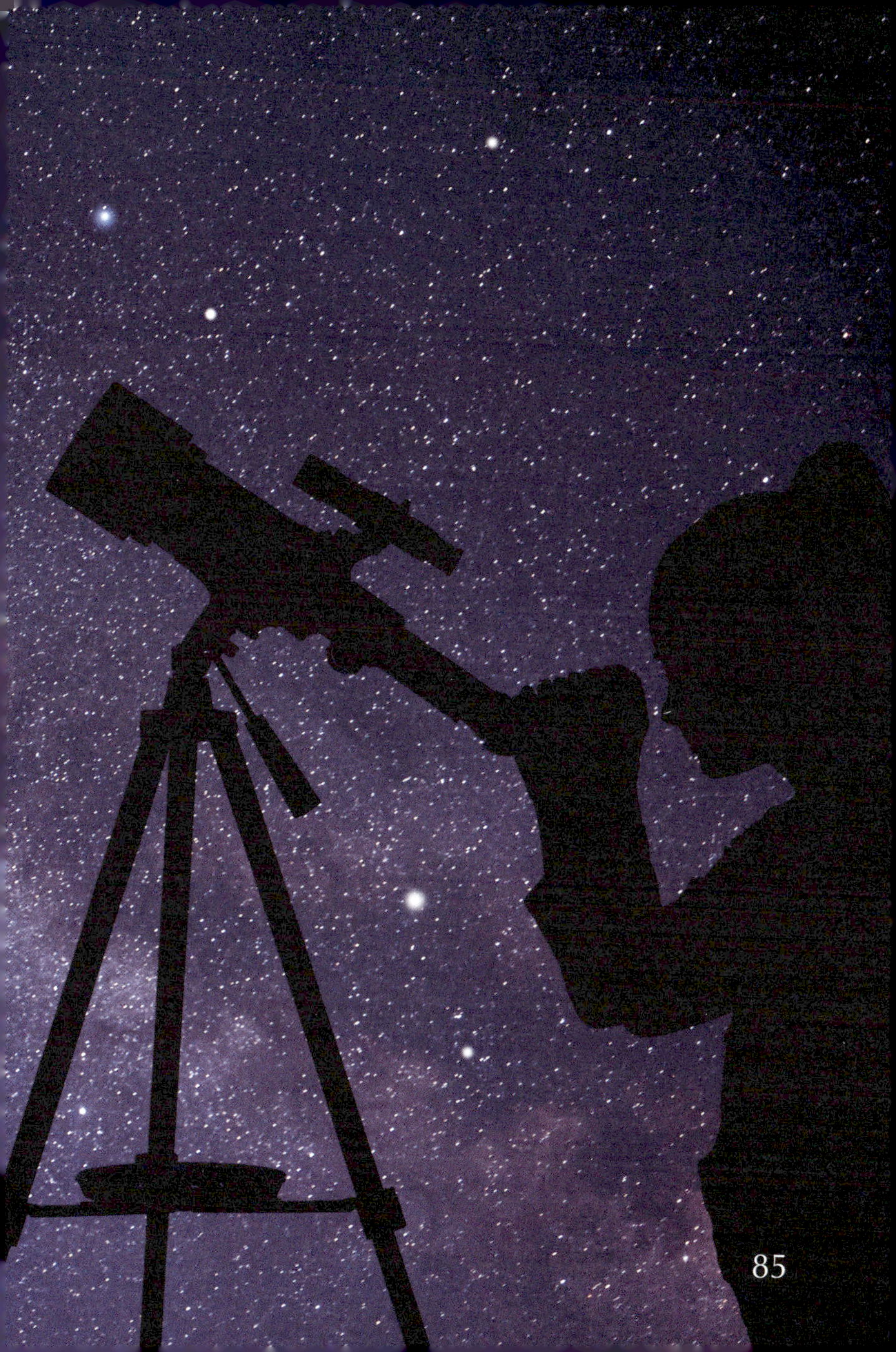

Bonus
Glowing nature

Not everything in nature reflects light. Here are some amazing living things that make their own light.

Bioluminescence is lots of tiny glowing animals in the sea.

glow-worms in a cave

glowing mushrooms

a comb jelly

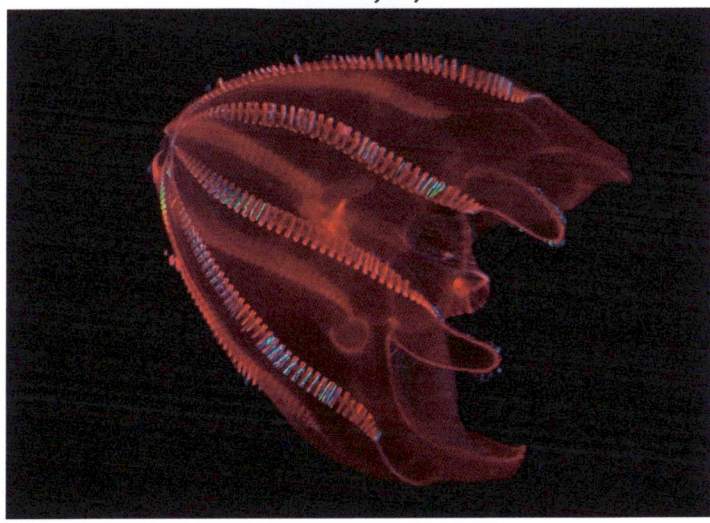

Chapter 6
Why does the Moon change shape?

The Sun is the brightest object in the sky, but at night it's the Moon that shines above us. Sometimes it's round, sometimes it's a semicircle, sometimes we can only see a tiny sliver of it. Why does the Moon change shape?

The Moon doesn't actually change shape. It's always sphere-shaped. What changes is how we see it from Earth.

First, let's start with some Moon facts.

Moon facts

The Moon is mostly made of rock.

The Moon's surface is covered in mountains and valleys, craters and dusty flat areas.

It's about a quarter of the size of Earth.

There are no signs of living things on the Moon.

At night, it is very cold – around −150 degrees Celsius – which is much colder than a kitchen freezer.

It is much closer to Earth than to the Sun.

The Moon can be scorching hot. Sometimes it is about 100 degrees Celsius, which is the temperature of boiling water.

In a spin

Like Earth and the other planets in our solar system, the Moon moves in two different ways. It rotates and it orbits.

The Moon spins round and round. Earth also rotates in the same way. You can't feel it spinning, but Earth is always moving.

At the same time as the Moon rotates, it also orbits. It takes about 27 days for the Moon to orbit Earth.

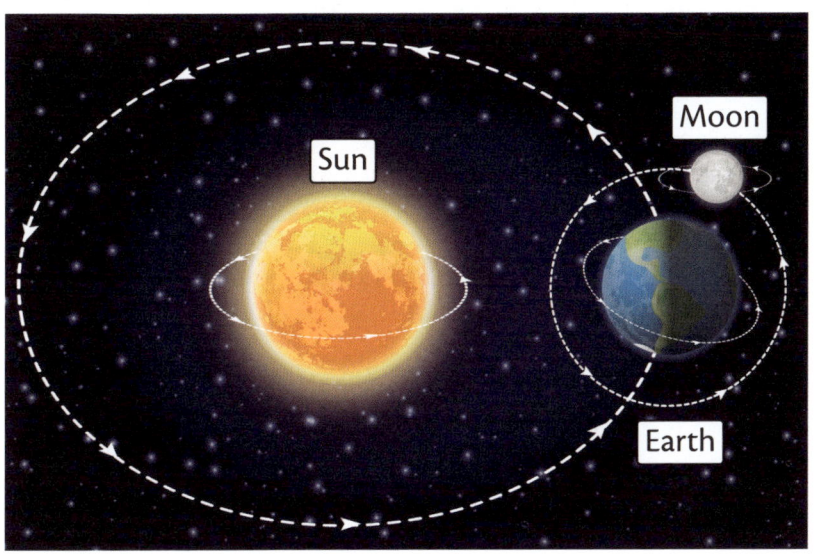

Phases of the Moon

The Moon doesn't make its own light. We see the Moon because it reflects light from the Sun, a bit like a mirror.

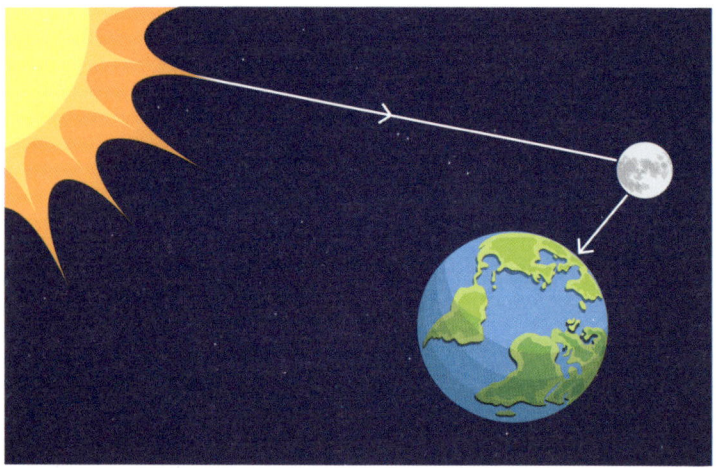

As the Moon travels around Earth, the Sun shines on the Moon's surface. We can only see the parts that are lit up by the Sun.

From Earth, the Moon looks like it changes shape gradually over the course of a month. Sometimes it looks like it's getting slightly bigger each day.

This is called 'waxing'. Sometimes it looks like it's getting slightly smaller each day. This is called 'waning'.

It's not only its size that changes. Its shape looks different too. Sometimes it's a full circle, sometimes it's a semicircle, sometimes it's like a C-shaped slice, sometimes it's hard to see it at all! These different shapes and sizes are called the phases of the Moon.

The first phase when we see the Moon is called 'waxing crescent'. The new Moon is actually invisible to us on Earth. As the Moon moves around Earth, the side facing us is gradually revealed. A full Moon is when the Moon is fully turned towards the Sun. At this time, we can see the side of the Moon that is facing Earth.

Each phase has a name. The phases are always in the same order.

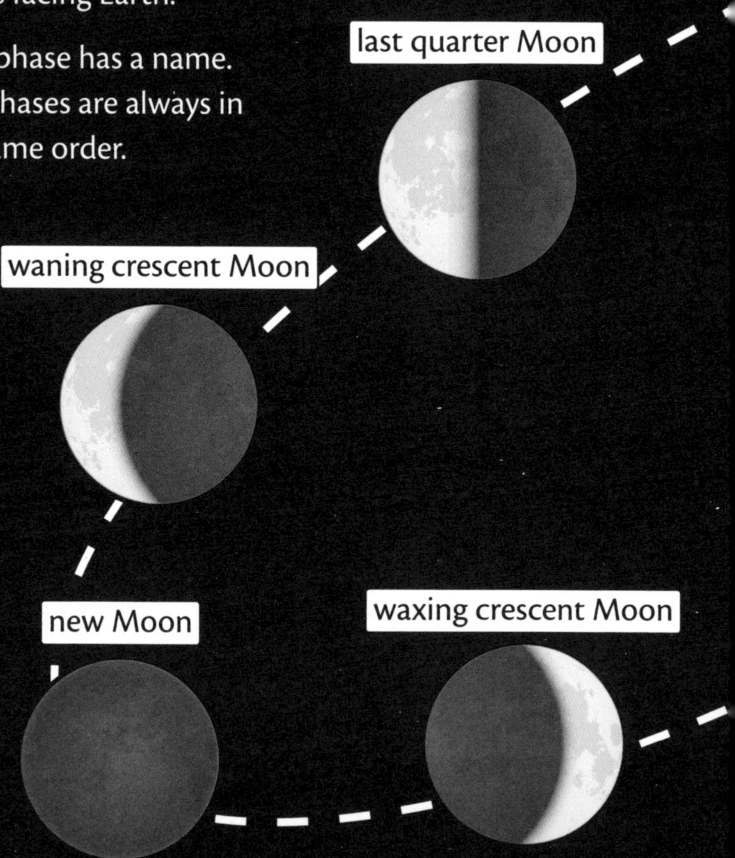
last quarter Moon
waning crescent Moon
new Moon
waxing crescent Moon

Did you know that each full moon has a different name through the year?

Many moons

Blood moon, blue moon, supermoon, harvest moon ... These are all different types of full moon.

A supermoon looks HUGE but, really, the moon isn't any bigger than normal. It just looks different to us because of its position in the sky. The Moon's orbit isn't a perfect circle. Its path is more oval-shaped. This means that sometimes the Moon is nearer to Earth, and other times it's further away.

We see a supermoon when the Moon is full and closest to Earth.

A blood moon looks like it's glowing red. It isn't really red. It's just reflecting red light in the atmosphere.

Daytime moon

When we imagine the Moon, we usually think of it shining in a dark, starry sky. So, it can be surprising to see the Moon during the day. We can sometimes see the Moon in the daytime when the Moon is in the correct position in the sky and it's reflecting enough light from the Sun. When the Moon is waning, you might see it in the morning. When the Moon is waxing, you can look out for it in the late afternoon, before sunset.

Eclipses

Solar eclipse

An eclipse happens when a planet or a moon blocks out the Sun's light. A solar eclipse happens when the Moon, the Sun and Earth are lined up in a way that means that the Moon blocks our view of the Sun. The Moon passes in front of the Sun and the Moon's shadow creeps across Earth, bringing darkness. When the Sun's light is completely blocked, the Moon looks like a black circle with a ring of fire around it.

Solar eclipses only happen when the Moon is in its new moon phase.

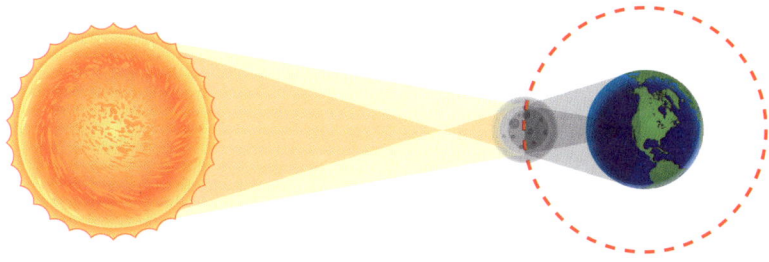

Did you know?

During a solar eclipse, it feels colder. Birds often stop singing. Animals might hide. In the past, people were afraid when there was an eclipse. They didn't understand why the sky suddenly went dark in the middle of the day.

 **Warning!**
Never look directly at the Sun or at a solar eclipse. It can damage your eyes.

Lunar eclipse

A lunar eclipse happens when Earth gets in between the Sun and the Moon and stops light from the Sun hitting the Moon. A lunar eclipse always happens during the full Moon phase.

When a lunar eclipse happens, Earth's shadow falls on the surface of the Moon. This can make the Moon fade to darkness, or sometimes it turns the Moon a bright red colour.

Earth seen from the Moon

We know what the Moon looks like from Earth, but what does Earth look like from the Moon? Thanks to Moon exploration, we know the answer.

One side of the Moon is always facing away from Earth – we call this the dark side of the Moon. If you were on this side of the Moon, you would never see Earth.

The other side of the Moon is always facing Earth. If you were on this side of the Moon, you would always see Earth. When viewed from the Moon, Earth stays in about the same spot in the sky all the time.

However, it doesn't always look exactly the same. As we know, the Moon orbits Earth and its orbit is oval-shaped. This means that sometimes Earth is closer to the Moon and appears larger. Sometimes it is further away and appears smaller.

Viewed from the Moon, Earth goes through phases, similar to the phases of the Moon. Earth's phases are directly opposite to the phases of the Moon seen from Earth. So, it would look a bit like this:

View from Earth	View from the Moon
new Moon ⟶	full Earth
full Moon ⟶	new Earth

How we see our Moon is always changing. It keeps us asking questions about the universe and our place in it. What questions will you ask the next time you look at the Moon?

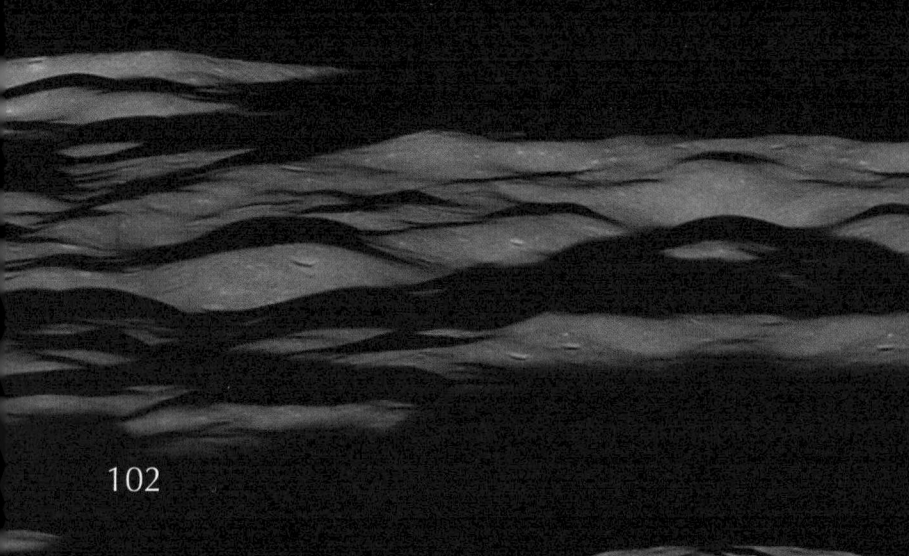

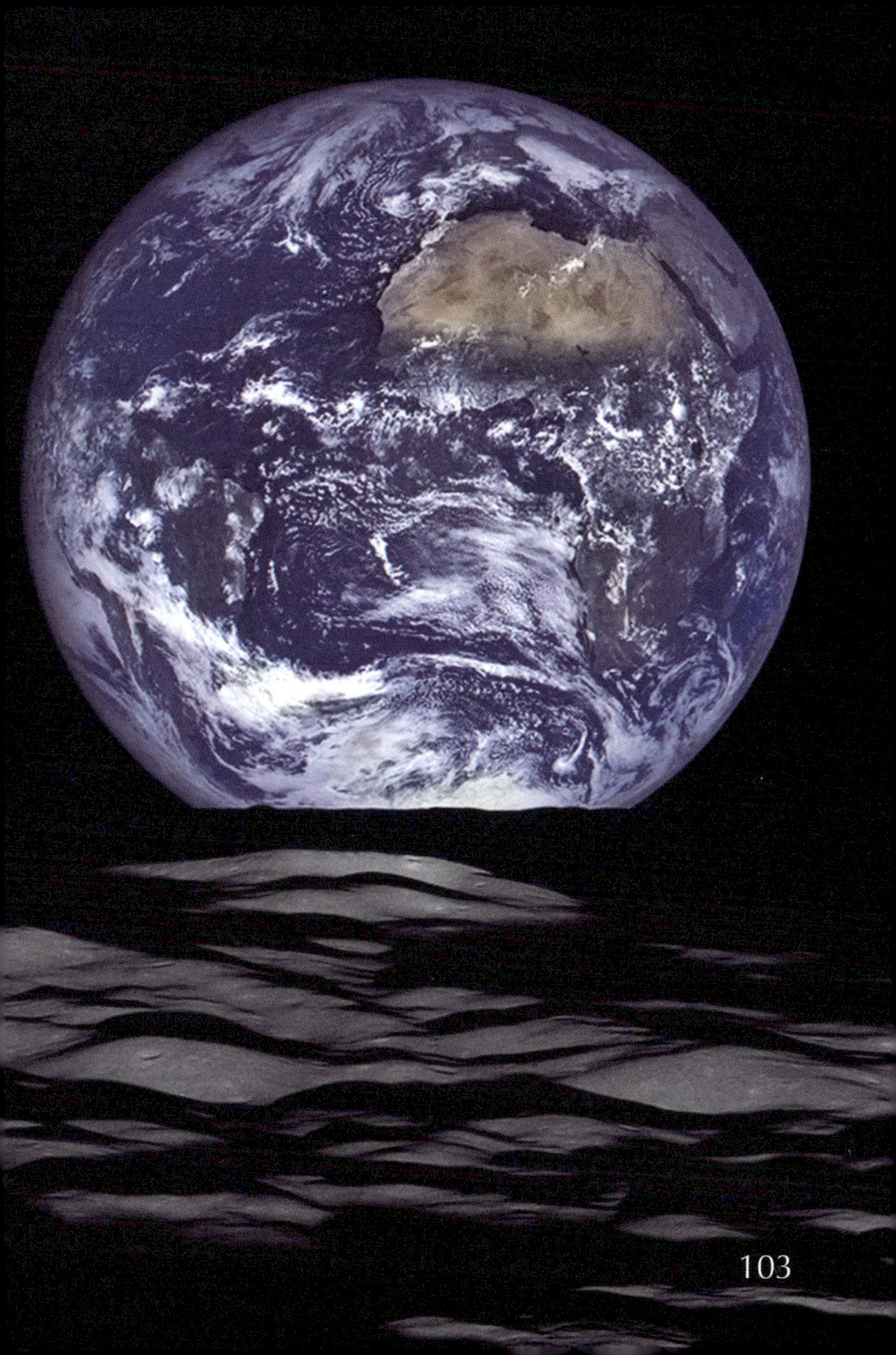

Glossary

atmosphere the mix of gases that surrounds Earth

carbon dioxide a gas breathed out by people and animals

continents very large areas of land, such as Europe or Africa

crater a large hole in the top of a volcano or on the moon

dilute mix with other liquids, like water

equator an imaginary line around the middle of Earth

evaporates water turns from a liquid to a gas

freshwater water that is not salty

glaciers large amounts of ice that move very slowly down a valley

gravity the force that pulls things towards the centre of Earth

lava hot liquid rock that comes out of volcanoes

light waves the form that light energy takes as it moves

magma very hot liquid rock found beneath Earth's surface

orbit a curved path of a planet or object as it moves around the Sun or another planet

oxygen a gas present in air and water

poles the most northern and southern points of Earth

solar system the Sun and all the planets moving around it

sphere an object shaped like a ball

universe the whole of space

vents holes that allow air, gas or liquid to escape

About the author

Did you always want to be an author?

I have always loved reading – I am a real bookworm! When I was little, I used to take a book with me wherever I went. I really enjoyed creative writing when I was at school, but at that point I never dreamed I could be an author myself. My first job was in a bookshop. Many years later, here I am writing books for children!

Hawys Morgan

What are your favourite sort of books to write?

I love writing books that teach me new things about the world. I learn a lot writing non-fiction books like this one. I learn lots when I write stories too. I always do plenty of research, so I feel like I fully understand the time, place and people in my stories.

How do you decide what to write about?

For me, the most important thing is to write about things that really interest me. Luckily, I'm interested in lots of different things, from ancient China to what lies beyond our solar system, so I'm never short of things to write about!

How did you come up with the idea for this book?

I came up with the idea thanks to my children. They're always asking questions that seem simple but, in reality, have complicated answers. There's nothing wrong with not knowing the answer to a question. What's important is that you try to find out the answer.

Did you know any of the answers already or did you have to do lots of research?

I thought I knew some of the answers. Then I started to research the book, and I discovered many things I thought I knew were wrong or didn't tell the whole story. In the end, I did lots of research!

What do you think is the most interesting thing in this book?

I think the most interesting thing about this book is that we actually can answer these big questions. From ancient Greek thinkers to modern scientists, people keep asking questions and using their amazing brains to work out the answers. Humans are incredible!

What do you hope readers will get from the book?

I hope it will inspire readers to ask their own big questions about the world around them and to find out the answers to those questions.

Are there more big questions you'd like to know the answers to?

How does the internet work? Who invented writing and why? How many ball games are there in the world? What inventions have changed the world? What's the smallest living creature … I could go on and on!

Book chat

What do you think of the title of this book?

Was there a particular question in this book you wanted to know the answer to?

Did you know any of the answers before reading the book?

What's the most interesting thing you've learnt from reading this book?

- What's the most surprising thing you've come across in this book?

- Are there some more big questions you want to know the answer to?

- If you could chat to the author, what would you ask?

- Do you have a favourite photograph in the book?

- If you had to make up a new title for the book, what would it be?

- Do you think there are some big questions we just don't know the answers to?

- Do you think there was a time in history when we had different answers or theories for these big questions?

- What would you like to learn even more about?

- Who would you recommend this book to and why?

Before you started reading, what did you think this book would be about? Did you change your mind as you read it?

Which of the big questions in the book did you find most interesting, and why?

Did you already know the answer to any of the questions?

Book challenge:

Come up with your own big question and do some research to see if you can find the answer to it.

Published by Collins
An imprint of HarperCollins*Publishers*

The News Building
1 London Bridge Street
London
SE1 9GF
UK

Macken House
39/40 Mayor Street Upper
Dublin 1
D01 C9W8
Ireland

© HarperCollins*Publishers* Limited 2025

Maps © Collins Bartholomew 2025

10 9 8 7 6 5 4 3 2 1

ISBN 978-0-00-876800-3

All rights reserved. No part of this publication may be reproduced, stored in a retrieval system, or transmitted in any form by any means, electronic, mechanical, photocopying, recording or otherwise, without the prior written permission of the Publisher or a licence permitting restricted copying in the United Kingdom issued by the Copyright Licensing Agency Ltd, 5th Floor, Shackleton House, 4 Battle Bridge Lane, London SE1 2HX.

Without limiting the exclusive rights of any author, contributor or the publisher of this publication, any unauthorised use of this publication to train generative artificial intelligence (AI) technologies is expressly prohibited. HarperCollins also exercise their rights under Article 4(3) of the Digital Single Market Directive 2019/790 and expressly reserve this publication from the text and data mining exception.

British Library Cataloguing-in-Publication Data
A catalogue record for this publication is available from the British Library.

Download the teaching notes and word cards to accompany this book at:
http://littlewandle.org.uk/signupfluency/

Get the latest Collins Big Cat news at
collins.co.uk/collinsbigcat

Author: Hawys Morgan
Publisher: Laura White
Commissioning editor and
    product manager: Caroline Green
Series editor: Charlotte Raby
Development editor: Catherine Baker
Project manager: Emily Hooton
Copyeditor: Sally Byford
Proofreader: Catherine Dakin
Cover designer: Sarah Finan
Typesetter: 2Hoots Publishing Services Ltd
Production controller: Katharine Willard

Printed in the UK.

 **MIX**
Paper | Supporting
responsible forestry
FSC
www.fsc.org   **FSC™ C007454**

This book contains FSC™ certified paper and other controlled sources to ensure responsible forest management.

For more information visit: www.harpercollins.co.uk/green

Made with responsibly sourced paper and vegetable ink

Scan to see how we are reducing our environmental impact.

Acknowledgements
The publishers gratefully acknowledge the permission granted to reproduce the copyright material in this book. Every effort has been made to trace copyright holders and to obtain their permission for the use of copyright material. The publishers will gladly receive any information enabling them to rectify any error or omission at the first opportunity.

Front cover t mspoint/Shutterstock, b Yashi S007/Shutterstock, p9 Dorling Kindersley ltd/Alamy, p10 Alexis Rosenfeld/Getty Images, p30t Dr Keith Wheeler/Science Photo Library, p31b Cat'chy Images/Alamy, pp34–35 Science History Images/Alamy, p35t NOAA/Alamy, p35c Solvin Zankl/Alamy, pp36–37 The Ocean Cleanup, p45 NASA Image Collection, p46 Science History Images/Alamy, p47 Science Photo Library, p56 Natalia Lukiianova/Alamy, p63 Universal Images Group North America LLC/Alamy, p68b CPA Media Pte Ltd/Alamy, p69tr peace portal photo/Alamy, p83 Wavebreak Media ltd/Alamy, p100 Apostoli Rossella/Getty Images, pp102–103 NASA.

All other photos Shutterstock.